THE ECON(
OF REPARA I IUN

WITH THE ESSAY
Reparations and Inter-Allied Debt
BY JOHN MAYNARD KEYNES

By

J. A. HOBSON

First published in 1915

This edition published by Read Books Ltd.
Copyright © 2019 Read Books Ltd.
This book is copyright and may not be
reproduced or copied in any way without
the express permission of the publisher in writing

British Library Cataloguing-in-Publication Data
A catalogue record for this book is available
from the British Library

CONTENTS

Reparations and Inter-Allied Debt 5

FOREWORD 11

I. REPARATION IN THE VERSAILLES TREATY 13

II. THE PARIS DEMANDS 18

III. THE ULTIMATUM TERMS 22

IV. CAPACITY TO PAY 29

V. ALLIED OBSTACLES TO REPARATIONS 32

VI. THE EXPORT SURPLUS 36

REPARATIONS
AND INTER-ALLIED DEBT

BY JOHN MAYNARD KEYNES
AN ESSAY FROM ESSAYS IN LIBERALISM

Mr. Keynes said:—I do not complain of Lord Balfour's Note, provided we assume, as I think we can, that it is our first move, and not our last. Many people seem to regard it as being really addressed to the United States. I do not agree. Essentially it is addressed to France. It is a reply, and a very necessary reply, to the kites which M. Poincaré has been flying in *The Times* and elsewhere, suggesting that this country should sacrifice all its claims of every description in return for—practically nothing at all, certainly not a permanent solution of the general problem. The Note brings us back to the facts and to the proper starting-point for negotiations.

In this question of Reparations the position changes so fast that it may be worth while for me to remind you just how the question stands at this moment. There are in existence two inconsistent settlements, both of which still hold good in law. The first is the assessment of the Reparation Commission, namely, 132 milliard gold marks. This is a capital sum. The second is the London Settlement, which is not a capital sum at all, but a schedule of annual payments calculated according to a formula; but the capitalised value of these annual payments, worked out on any reasonable hypothesis, comes to much less than the Reparation Commission's total, probably to not much more than a half.

THE BREAKDOWN OF GERMANY

But that is not the end of the story. While both the above settlements remain in force, the temporary régime under which Germany has been paying is different from, and much less than, either of them. By a decision of last March Germany was to pay during 1922 £36,000,000 (gold) in cash, *plus* deliveries in kind. The value of the latter cannot be exactly calculated, but, apart from coal, they do not amount to much, with the result that the 1922 demands are probably between a third and a quarter of the London Settlement, and less than one-sixth of the Reparation Commission's original total. It is under the weight of this reduced burden that Germany has now broken down, and the present crisis is due to her inability to continue these reduced instalments beyond the payment of July, 1922. In the long run the payments due during 1922 should be within Germany's capacity. But the insensate policy pursued by the Allies for the last four years has so completely ruined her finances, that for the time being she can pay nothing at all; and for a shorter or longer period it is certain that there is now no alternative to a moratorium.

What, in these circumstances, does M. Poincaré propose? To judge from the semi-official forecasts, he is prepared to cancel what are known as the "C" Bonds, provided Great Britain lets France off the whole of her debt and forgoes her own claims to Reparation. What are these "C" Bonds? They are a part of the London Settlement of May, 1921, and, roughly speaking, they may be said to represent the excess of the Reparation Commission's assessment over the capitalised value of the London Schedule of Payments, and a bit more. That is to say, they are pure water. They mainly represent that part of the Reparation Commission's total assessment which will not be covered, even though the London Schedule of Payments is paid in full.

In offering the cancellation of these Bonds, therefore, M. Poincaré is offering exactly nothing. If Great Britain gave up her own claims to Reparations, and the "C" Bonds were cancelled to the extent of France's indebtedness to us, France's claims against Germany would be actually greater, even on paper, than they are now. For the demands under the London Settlement would be unabated, and France would be entitled to a larger proportion of them. The offer is, therefore, derisory. And it seems to me to be little short of criminal on the part of *The Times* to endeavour to trick the people of this country into such a settlement.

Personally, I do not think that at this juncture there is anything whatever to be done except to grant a moratorium. It is out of the question that any figure, low enough to do Germany's credit any good now, could be acceptable to M. Poincaré, in however moderate a mood he may visit London next week. Apart from which, it is really impossible at the present moment for any one to say how much Germany will be able to pay in the long run. Let us content ourselves, therefore, with a moratorium for the moment, and put off till next year the discussion of a final settlement, when, with proper preparations beforehand, there ought to be a grand Conference on the whole connected problem of inter-Governmental debt, with representatives of the United States present, and possibly at Washington.

THE ILLUSION OF A LOAN

The difficulties in the way of any immediate settlement now are so obvious that one might wonder why any one should be in favour of the attempt. The explanation lies in that popular illusion, with which it now pleases the world to deceive itself— the International Loan. It is thought that if Germany's liability can now be settled once and for all, the "bankers" will then lend her a huge sum of money by which she can anticipate her liabilities and satisfy the requirements of France.

In my opinion the International Loan on a great scale is just as big an illusion as Reparations on a great scale. It will not happen. It cannot happen. And it would make a most disastrous disturbance if it did happen. The idea that the rest of the world is going to lend to Germany, for her to hand over to France, about 100 per cent. of their liquid savings—for that is what it amounts to—is utterly preposterous. And the sooner we get that into our heads the better. I am not quite clear for what sort of an amount the public imagine that the loan would be, but I think the sums generally mentioned vary from £250,000,000 up to £500,000,000. The idea that any Government in the world, or all of the Governments in the world in combination, let alone bankrupt Germany, could at the present time raise this amount of new money (that is to say, for other purposes than the funding or redemption of existing obligations) from investors in the world's Stock Exchanges is ridiculous.

The highest figure which I have heard mentioned by a reliable authority is £100,000,000. Personally, I think even this much too high. It could only be realised if subscriptions from special quarters, as, for example, German hoards abroad, and German-Americans, were to provide the greater part of it, which would only be the case if it were part of a settlement which was of great and obvious advantage to Germany. A loan to Germany, on Germany's own credit, yielding, say, 8 to 10 per cent., would not in my opinion be an investor's proposition in any part of the world, except on a most trifling scale. I do not mean that a larger anticipatory loan of a different character—issued, for example, in Allied countries with the guarantees of the Allied Government, the proceeds in each such country being handed over to the guaranteeing Government, so that no new money would pass—might not be possible. But a loan of this kind is not at present in question.

Yet a loan of from £50,000,000 to £100,000,000—and I repeat that even this figure is very optimistic except as the result of a settlement of a kind which engaged the active goodwill of individual Germans with foreign resources and of foreigners of German origin and sympathies—would only cover Germany's liabilities under the London Schedule for four to six months, and the temporarily reduced payments of last March for little more than a year. And from such a loan, after meeting Belgian priorities and Army of Occupation costs, there would not be left any important sum for France.

I see no possibility, therefore, of any final settlement with M. Poincaré in the immediate future. He has now reached the point of saying that he is prepared to talk sense in return for an enormous bribe, and that is some progress. But as no one is in a position to offer him the bribe, it is not much progress, and as the force of events will compel him to talk sense sooner or later, even without a bribe, his bargaining position is not strong. In the meantime he may make trouble. If so, it can't be helped. But it will do him no good, and may even help to bring nearer the inevitable day of disillusion. I may add that for France to agree to a short moratorium is not a great sacrifice since, on account of the Belgian priority and other items, the amount of cash to which France will be entitled in the near future, even if the payments fixed last March were to be paid in full, is quite trifling.

A POLICY FOR THE LIBERAL PARTY

So much for the immediate situation and the politics of the case. If we look forward a little, I venture to think that there is a clear, simple, and practical policy for the Liberal Party to adopt and to persist in. Both M. Poincaré and Mr. Lloyd George have their hands tied by their past utterances. Mr. Lloyd George's part in the matter of Reparations is the most discreditable episode in his career. It is not easy for him, whose hands are not clean in the matter, to give us a clean settlement. I say this although his present intentions appear to be reasonable. All the more reason why others should pronounce and persist in a clear and decided policy. I was disappointed, if I may say so, in what Lord Grey had to say about this at Newcastle last week. He said many wise things, but not a word of constructive policy which could get any one an inch further forward. He seemed to think that all that was necessary was to talk to the French sympathetically and to put our trust in international bankers. He puts a faith in an international loan as the means of solution which I am sure is not justified. We must be much more concrete than that, and we must be prepared to say unpleasant things as well as pleasant ones.

The right solution, the solution that we are bound to come to in the end, is not complicated. We must abandon the claim for pensions and bring to an end the occupation of the Rhinelands. The Reparation Commission must be asked to divide their assessment into two parts—the part that represents pensions and separation allowances and the rest. And with the abandonment of the former the proportion due to France would be correspondingly raised. If France would agree to this—which is in her interest, anyhow—and would terminate the occupation it would be right for us to forgive her (and our other Allies) all they owe us, and to accord a priority on all receipts in favour of the devastated areas. If we could secure a real settlement by these sacrifices, I think we should make them completely regardless of what the United States may say or do.

In declaring for this policy in the House of Commons yesterday, Mr. Asquith has given the Liberal Party a clear lead. I hope that they will make it a principal plank in their platform. This is a just and honourable settlement, satisfactory to sentiment and to expediency. Those who adopt it unequivocally will find that they have with them the tide and a favouring wind. But no one must suppose that, even with such a settlement, any important part of Germany's payments can be anticipated by a loan. Any small loan that can be raised will be required for Germany herself, to put her on her legs again, and enable her to make the necessary annual payments.

FOREWORD

As a result of the International Conference held in London in November 1920, at the instance of the Fight the Famine Council, a Peace Revision Committee was formed, of which I was appointed Chairman. The material and arguments presented here were originally intended for submission to this Committee, but the difficulties and delay of communication with foreign members were such as to induce me to publish it under my own name and upon my sole responsibility as a contribution to the discussion of a matter which vitally concerns the peace and economic recovery of Europe.

J. A. H.

June 21, 1921.

I

REPARATION IN THE VERSAILLES TREATY

THE pre-armistice agreement under which Germany laid down her arms in November 1918 contained the following provision for reparation :

"The President declared that invaded territories must be restored as well as evacuated and freed. The Allied Governments feel that no doubt ought to be allowed to exist as to what this provision implies. By it they understand that compensation will be made by Germany for all damage done to the civilian population of the Allies and their property by the aggression of Germany by land, by sea, and from the air."

When the question came up for settlement in the terms of the Versailles Treaty, Mr. J. F. Dulles, addressing the Supreme Council on behalf of the American delegates, recorded their judgment that

The foregoing language constitutes, in so far as reparation is concerned, the terms upon which the United States and the Allies agree to make peace with Germany and the terms upon which Germany accepted the armistice on November 11, 1918.

To this category of reparation the American delegates added another, not expressly laid down in the Wilson declaration, but held by them to be inherently right and unaffected by those declarations, viz. that " Reparation is due for all damage directly consequent upon acts of the enemy clearly in violation of international law, as recognized at the time of the commission of the acts in question." How much would have been added to the sum of reparation by such compensation, properly assessed before an impartial international tribunal, and offset by any similar compensation for violation of international law that may have been committed by Allies, it is of course impossible to compute. But it may be held certain that any assessment of these two sorts of reparations (or probably of the first alone) would amount to a sum at least equal to Germany's total ability to pay, as determined by any fair consideration of her available resources.

The Americans, however, held that the proposal, pressed by the British and the French delegates, for the inclusion in reparations of the entire " costs of the war," as distinct from these defined damages, was a plain violation of the pledge of the pre-armistice agreement. Those who agreed to the case for the extension, relied (in particular the French) upon the terms of the armistice agreement of November 11, 1918, which contained clause 19, opening thus : " With the reservation that any future claims and demands of the Allies and the United States of America remain unaffected, the following financial conditions are imposed : Reparation for damage done." This general reservation, made subsequently to the pre-armistice arrangement, they contended, left the Allies free to present any claims for reparation they thought fit. The American rejoinder to the effect that the armistice terms were " A military document, designed only to ensure the Allies being in a position to enforce the peace arrangements previously entered into," and in nowise competent to modify or over-ride the earlier agreement, was for some time not accepted by the members of the Supreme Council who stood for the inclusion of " war costs." Nothing short of the instruction of President Wilson that the American delegates should dissent " and, if necessary, dissent openly " from a procedure " which is clearly inconsistent with what we deliberately led the enemy to expect and cannot now honourably alter simply because we have the power," [1] stopped the Supreme Council from this flagrant violation of their pre-armistice pledge. But, formally bowing to the American protest, the other members of the Council reinstated a large section of their claim under the head of " actual damage." For in Article 232 of the Versailles Treaty we read : " The Allied and Associated Governments, however, require and Germany undertakes, that she will make compensation for all damage done to the civilian population of the Allies and Associated Powers and to their property during the period of the belligerency of each as an Allied or Associated Power against Germany by such aggression by land, by sea, and from the air, *and in general all damage as defined in Annex* 1, *hereto.*" Now while the body of this clause conforms to the pre-armistice agreement, its tail contains violations as patent and almost as substantial as that of the proposal to include the entire " war costs " under reparations. For, on turning to Annex 1 we find the whole of

[1] Baruch, p. 25.

" pensions and separation allowances " brought under reparations on the ground (adduced in a memorandum by General Smuts) that they came under the head of " damage to the civilian population of the Allies in their person and properties which resulted from the German aggression." Now any reasonable reading of this Smuts memorandum makes it evident that it validates the full French claim for including the entire cost of the war, and that its logic involves that the whole of the Allied war expenditure met by taxation and loans, including the interest hereafter to be paid in all war-borrowing, should form a claim for reparation.

" What had really happened," writes Mr. Baruch, " was a compromise between the Prime Minister's pledge to the British electorate to claim the entire costs of the war, and the pledge to the contrary which the Allies had given to Germany at the Armistice." [1]

But this extension of the pre-armistice reparations to include pensions, allowances, and other *indirect damages* to civilians, by no means exhausts the violations of the earlier agreement, contained in Annex 1. The provision that Germany shall be responsible for the reparation in respect of civilian damage done by her Allies is equally indefensible. This illicit extension of the claim on Germany was doubtless due, in part, to the fact that the other Allies could not be regarded as capable of any financial reparation, in part, to the desire of certain representatives of the Allies to load on to Germany a completely crushing burden of indemnity.

The failure to fix the total amount of reparation Germany was called upon to pay was an almost necessary implication of these violations of the pre-armistice agreement. Difficult as was the task of assessing fairly the material damage sustained by the inhabitants of the invaded areas, by partial commissions naturally sympathetic with the sufferers and therefore lenient in their scrutiny of claims, an approximately correct estimate of this damage might have given a sum admittedly within the capacity of Germany to pay. The addition of these vast new obligations of unfathomable magnitude rendered it virtually impossible to reach a figure measuring the total damages for which reparation should be claimed. Any such figure would be recognized as of purely speculative value and its magnitude might have been such as to evoke that reasonable scrutiny of Germany's " ability to pay " which it was deemed politically expedient at this stage to postpone. For, as will presently be shown, any serious attempt to check the " costs " or " damages " basis of reparation, by this consideration

[1] Baruch, p. 157

15

been kept, it might have been feasible to assess the total reparations on a basis of proved damages, but the inclusion of Pensions, Allowances and other immeasurably great items in Annex 1, would yield a result so far in excess of Germany's actual or potential capacity to pay, as to render such a process of assessment nugatory. It might, therefore, be taken as generally admitted, that the real problem is that of ascertaining the maximum amount which Germany can afford to pay and the Allies to receive from her. The importance of this latter qualification will appear a little later on. The first question is that of measuring Germany's capacity to pay. But before proceeding to discuss such measures it is important to recognize two guiding principles laid down for instruction to the Reparation Commission.

The first is that reparation should have due regard to the economic life of Germany. In the interpretative note to Germany of June 16, 1919, the Allied and Associated Powers made the following declaration :

" The resumption of German industry involves access by the German people to food supplies, and by the German manufacturers to the necessary raw materials and provision for their transport to Germany from overseas. The resumption of German industry is an interest of the Allied and Associated Powers as well as an interest of Germany. They are fully alive to the fact, and therefore declare that they will not withhold from Germany commercial facilities without which this resumption cannot take place, but that, subject to conditions and within limits, which cannot be laid down in advance, and subject also to the necessity of having due regard for the special economic situation created for Allied and Associated countries by German aggression and the war, they are prepared to afford to Germany facilities in these directions for the common good." [1]

The second guiding principle is that the performance of the reparation by Germany should be secured, if possible, " within a period of thirty years from May 1, 1921,[2] though it remains within the discretion of the Commission to postpone for settlement in subsequent years " any balance remaining unpaid." To this latter provision Mr. Baruch, however, appends the following brief commentary : " From a practical standpoint, the present value of a sum payable without interest after thirty years is very small. To have required interest payments on sums due after thirty years would have meant the practical impossibility of ever discharging the principal of the debt."[3]

[1] Baruch, p. 58.   [2] Article 233.   [3] Baruch, p. 60.

*

17

THE ECONOMICS OF REPARATION

II

THE PARIS DEMANDS

THIS recital of the treatment of the reparation problem from the time of the pre-armistice agreement to the insertion of the reparation clauses in the Versailles Treaty has been necessary in order to bring out the four radical defects in all subsequent attempts at a settlement of the issue. The first is the violation of the pre-armistice agreement limiting the sort of damage for which reparation should be made. The second is the procedure by assessment of the extended damages without close regard to ability to pay. The third is the unjudicial and necessarily erroneous assessment of damages and of modes for payment by a partial tribunal. The fourth is the failure of the Allies to undertake to give the industrial, commercial and financial conditions rendering payment possible. The cumulative effect of these initial errors is seen in each stage of the proceedings to enforce the reparation clauses. The basis of computation and the time conditions laid down in the treaty were such as ruled out from the start any possibility of fulfilment on the part of Germany. Any payments in kind, or allied expenses to be defrayed by Germany, were to be determined arbitrarily by one interested party. The value of deliveries in kind, such as coal, ships, engines, was liable to be depressed by the enforcement of their delivery at a more rapid rate than the economic needs of the recipients required. This policy had the further necessary effect of injuring the productive power of Germany, and so reducing her general ability to make subsequent payments of reparation.

The failure of Germany to satisfy the first demand for the payment of £1,000,000,000 in gold values by May 1, 1921, was made inevitable by these conditions. The amount of Germany's net payment could be reduced by bloating the costs of the Armies of Occupation or by the low valuation of the goods delivered. The former process was inevitable when the military authorities of the occupied areas had no inducement to keep down expenses. In point of fact the payment for an American private soldier approximated to the salary of a general in the German forces, and it was notorious that most of the luxuries in these areas which figured in our Press as evidence of German wealth were for the exclusive use of the Allied soldiery. But the fundamental injustice and irra-

18

tionality of the claim to be a judge in one's own cause comes out in the valuation of the deliveries. Germany claimed to have delivered, after due allowances, the full sum of £1,000,000,000. The Reparation Commission assessed these deliveries at £400,000,000. A large part of this wide difference was by admission due to the fact that the Germans valued at the time of delivery, the Commission at a later period when values had fallen, chiefly owing to the very size of those deliveries of coal, ships, dyes, etc., in the face of a shrinking market. But, quite apart from this consideration, lay the natural tendency of the two parties to value in accordance with their respective interests. In no important private business bargain would it be deemed possible to get a fair valuation by the method laid down in the Versailles Treaty. This violation of the elementary principle of equity poisons the whole reparation question, making any pacific settlement impossible. For the Treaty provision by which Germany was compelled to admit the judgment of her enemies as final in all disagreements as to fulfilment of demands, is nothing other than an indefinite continuance of the rule of force in peace-time. As time goes on it will become continuously more evident that there can be no security for Europe until the question of fulfilment of the reparation and all other conditions of the Treaty has been removed from the arbitrament of one of the interested parties and put under the jurisdiction of a genuinely international tribunal.

The inherent injustice and unreason of the method pursued in its bearing on reparation are evinced in the refusal to take as the basis of actual demand an objective view of Germany's ability to pay. Seeing that by the illicit additions made to the pre-armistice bill, the war damages against Germany (however fairly assessed) must greatly exceed the early capacity of Germany, it might have seemed reasonable that the Allies should have done their utmost to explore, test and value, that capacity, and should have striven to adjust their demands to it. But no such thing. Political considerations required the Allied Governments to maintain the position that Germany was to be made to pay the war expenses, and that vast sums would be recovered from her to lighten the Allied debts and restore their finances. Politics disinclined them for any closer scrutiny of the economic sources from which these phantom billions were to be drawn. When driven into a corner they committed themselves to quite fantastic calculations, without relation either to the power of Germany to pay, the willingness of the Allies to receive such payment, or to the terms of their own Treaty under which they professed to act. Of such a character were the Paris demands of January 1921. These demands required, first, the payment of fixed annuities to the following amounts :

100 millions £ per annum for the first 2 years from May 1921.
150 ,, ,, next 3 years.
200 ,, ,, ,, 3 years.
250 ,, ,, ,, 3 years.
300 ,, ,, following 31 years.

The sum of these 42 annual payments is 11,300 million £, or, at their discounted present value, some 5,500 million £. But to these payments of fixed amount are added 42 payments " equal to 12 per cent. ad valorem of Germany's exports."

How much this 12 per cent. on export would have added to the fixed annuities, it is of course impossible to estimate with precision. But one admitted economic truth enables us to make an approximate calculation. The total net annual payments for reparation must be represented in an excess of export over import values. For in no other way can the payment in gold marks or world currency be met. Now German export trade requires an import trade to furnish the foreign raw materials without which most of the staple exports, e.g. metal goods and textiles, could not be produced, and to supply the deficits in goods and materials needed for the support of the working population. Though no closely fixed proportion exists between this import trade and the export trade, every increase of the latter will involve an increase of the former in some proportionate scale. Mr. Keynes shows reasons for holding that it is impossible to suppose that " Germany could continuously maintain her exports at a value of more than, say, 40 per cent. above her imports." Upon such a basis the payment of the earliest and lowest of the annuities, with the 12 per cent., would involve a total export trade of nearly 700 million £ with an import trade of 500 millions, yielding surplus imports approaching 200 millions, a sum enough to pay a fixed 116 millions with the 12 per cent. tax of 84 millions. Every fresh step in the increase of fixed payments would, of course, entail a corresponding increase of the tax amount, until after eleven years the high level of an aggregate annual payment of about 400 millions £ would be reached.

Having regard to the facts that the export trade of Germany in 1920 did not reach one-half of the 700 millions £ which Mr. Keynes holds normally sufficient to support the payment of the first of the annual demands, while the trade balance for the year exhibited a surplus not of exports but of imports, the Paris demands seem to be impracticable at their start. But suppose that by a special financial effort, such as the sale or mortgage of internal capital resources, the earlier payments could be made, is it credible that in eleven years' time provision could be made for the annual payment over a period of thirty-one years of such a sum as 400 millions ? Can anybody contemplate the economic situation in which year after year so vast a tribute could pour out of Germany into the Allied countries, flooding their markets ? The very thought of such a predicament was enough to evoke plans of a most determined kind for keeping out these goods by all the nations threatened with such bounties. If the bad exchange of Germany sufficed to drive a " free trade " people like ours into protective legislation, before the era of indemnities began, what would happen when the manufacturers and traders of the several Allied nations saw their own reparation policy impelling Germany to undersell their own products not only in neutral markets but in their home markets, in order to pay the annual instalments of the reparation ?

At first the Allied politicians tried to wriggle out of the predicament by futile proposals to demand payments in exports of raw materials which Germany was to find either out of her own national resources or, as must inevitably be the case, out of other countries into which she was to be free to " dump " the cheap manufactures we could not consent to receive. But though this seemed a satisfactory way out to Mr. Lloyd George, our business men saw that nothing would be gained by keeping German manufactured goods out of our markets, if these same goods were going to oust us from all the neutral markets of the world and often to invade our markets in the disguise of finished neutral commodities.

But, finally, suppose that the Allies had been willing and able to receive these huge supplies of unpaid exports, and to adjust their economic systems to the regular gratuities, what would happen when the 42 years came to a close, and the parasites were suddenly robbed of their accustomed prey ? One has only to state the problem in order to show how incredible it is that this scheme of Paris should have received support of any economic authorities. Quite manifestly it emanated from the disordered brains of politicians not concerned with facts or their consequences, but with keeping up appearances and feeding the passions and credulity of their people.

But before proceeding to discuss the latest form of the reparation demands, it may be well to point out that the Paris demands, and the situation to which they gave rise, were as illegal in form as they were foolish and impracticable in substance.

Article 233 of the Treaty empowered not the Supreme Council, but the Reparation Commission, to determine the amount of the reparation, to notify it to the German Government " on or before May 1921," and to " draw up a schedule for securing and discharging the entire obligation within a period of thirty years from May 1, 1921." The Supreme Council substituted for the Reparation Commission their own unauthorized will, infringed their own instructions to that body by adding to the fixed payments demanded an indeterminate body of taxation, extended the period of payment to forty-two years, and enforced these demands at once instead of waiting for the default of Germany. Moreover, the " sanctions " they applied are not in accordance with the provision of this part of the Treaty. For the Allies had themselves laid down explicitly in the Versailles Treaty the method of procedure for determining the amount of the reparation and for arranging its payment. It provides that, in the event of Germany's failure to make payment, the Commission may postpone the payment or that " such other action may be taken as the Allied and Associated Governments, acting in accordance with the procedure laid down in this part of the present Treaty, shall determine." This makes it clear that such changes in the terms of reparation, and in the methods of enforcement, lay entirely outside the competence of the Supreme Council and could only be made by the Commission or by the Allied Powers as a whole, in co-operation with the United States of America.

III

THE ULTIMATUM TERMS

THOSE who have complacently assumed that the reparation issue has at last been brought to a satisfactory settlement by Germany's acceptance of the latest decision of the Reparation Commission (communicated to her by the Supreme Council under the cover of an Ultimatum) are the dupes of external formalities that ignore or hide the really relevant considerations. Neither the decision of the Reparation Commission nor the German acceptance takes due account of what we must recognize to be the determinant factor of the issue, Germany's capacity to pay. The decision merely reiterates Germany's liability under the Treaty to pay the damages assessed to her, and lays out the methods and times for payment. Capacity to pay, so far as taken into account at all, is assumed,

ERRATA

Page 15, line 18, *read* "billions" *for* "millions."

Page 15, line 24, *read* "£5,500,000,000" *for* "£5,500,000."

Page 15, line 40, *read* "millions" *after* "£100."

THE ECONOMICS OF REPARATION

not proved. Nor can Germany's acceptance be taken as presumptive proof of her capacity. It is common knowledge that the signature of Germany to the latest Allied demands was extorted by the threat of an immediate invasion which would lead to the political disruption of the nation and its economic destruction. It involves no imputation of ill faith to any unarmed person or community that they should put their name to any undertaking, however impossible to fulfilment, that is thus presented to them at the cannon's mouth. There exists neither moral nor legal obligation to carry out an undertaking thus extorted by force, even were it practically feasible. Where fulfilment is not feasible, the issue of obligation does not arise at all. Those who would understand the real significance of this latest phase of the reparation issue, must look beneath the political moves and motives to the economic bedrock.

In form the new demands are less unreasonable than those of Paris, and are in closer accordance with the Treaty terms. They fix the total liability at the sum of 137 millions of gold marks (inclusive of the payment due May 1, and the Belgian debt to the Allies) or £6,850,000,000. Towards this sum Germany is estimated to have paid £100,000,000, after discharging the food credits and the costs of the armies of occupation in accordance with Treaty provisions. This total, though considerably larger than the fixed part of the Paris demands (£5,500,000), is probably less than the Paris sum increased by the value of the indeterminate yield of the 12 per cent. export duty. For though the Ultimatum demands raised the export duty to 26 per cent., this adds nothing to the final aggregate, which takes the changing yield of the tax into account.

The time-distribution of the payment is in certain respects better, in others worse, than that of Paris. Germany is to deliver bonds amounting to £600,000,000 by July 1, 1921, followed by £1,900,000,000 by November 1921. These bonds are to be issued at once to the investing public, on a 5 per cent. interest basis, and Germany is to provide this interest with a sinking fund of 1 per cent. in gold bonds, payable twice a year to the Allies and secured by a lien upon Customs and Export duties, or in default, upon all other properties of the German Government. The interest service of these two issues of bonds (amounting in all to £2,500,000,000) at 6 per cent. is £150,000,000. To meet this annual charge Germany must find a regular fixed contribution of £100 *plus* 26 per cent. of the total value of her exports. This export tax is thus assumed to yield at the start not less than £50,000,000, any yield in excess of that amount going to the sinking fund.

25

The remainder of the total sum, viz. £4,250,000,000, is to be provided by a third series of gold bonds, to be delivered next year to the Allied Governments, but only to be issued and put upon the market when the Reparation Commission decides that Germany's resources are adequate to meet the additional service of these bonds. Since there is to be no accumulation of interest in respect of this third series until it is actually issued, any reasonable view of the situation may leave out of account two-thirds of the total sum, which doubtless has a political use to pacify the popular demand for swinging damages, but no economic significance, since the time for its ripening into actuality is unlikely ever to be reached.

The necessity for postponement of the issue of the third series of bonds is pretty obvious. Their service would at once load the annual reparation payments with an additional £300,000,000 to provide the 6 per cent. interest and 1 per cent. sinking fund required for their service, a manifestly absurd proposal.

I am of opinion that the evidence of Germany's capacity to pay will make it clear that the Commission can never declare the arrival of the time for the issue of the £4,250,000,000 bonds, and that the Allied Governments must be aware of this fact and in view of the situation have decided, while maintaining the appearance of fulfilling their pledges to secure from Germany the full damages under the Treaty, to cut down their real demands to the figure, £2,500,000,000, which was the amount of Germany's alternative offer at Paris. This offer they rejected as derisory and unworthy of consideration. But though ill-formulated and not fully comprehensible in the form in which it was stated, it probably approximated to the truth in respect of Germany's capacity to pay, and the Allied reversion to this sum as the limit for their actual demands is a half-conscious testimony to the economic validity of that offer.

But though upon this hypothesis we may rule out the substance of the large postponed sum, its formal existence none the less operates very detrimentally upon the realities of reparation. The truly urgent need is the provision now of a large capital sum in order to set about without delay the reconstruction of the devastated areas. A protracted series of annual payments do not meet this need. Hence the proposal to put upon the world market the gold bonds to be paid this year by Germany to the Allies. Real reparation hinges upon the sale of these bonds in large amounts and at something like their full nominal value. Such a market in its turn depends upon the belief of the investing public in various countries, especially in America and the few other countries with funds available for such investments, that Germany can and will carry out her undertakings in respect to the service of these bonds. Now, while most men of financial experience will agree that, under renewed conditions of economic stability, and with fair access to external markets, Germany might with reasonable confidence be expected to be able to provide interest and sinking fund for a reparation of £2,500,000,000, they will refuse to entertain a proposition to provide the capital for such a fund, if there is attached to it the huge further obligation. For they will rightly judge that, whereas Germany might well exert its best energies to pay a sum that is within its compass, it will not do so, if success in that achievement is to be the test and cause for further and far larger demands upon her future energies. It may be replied, that if, as I have here argued, there is no serious expectation or intention on the part of the Allied Governments to extort this third issue, the damaging reaction on investors in the earlier issues should not arise. But everybody knows that the general investor, who is invited to assume this burden, is timid and suspicious, and that the formal existence of this large immeasurable risk is certain to operate most potently upon his timidity and suspicion in the case of an investment whose value is based upon German undertakings and assets. It is safe, therefore, to assert that no priority of claim upon the German assets for the first two issues will under these circumstances suffice to make them marketable except in small amounts and at exceedingly low prices. This will mean that the capital sums required for the early restoration of the devastated areas will not be forthcoming. Though part of this deficiency may be made up from such deliveries in kind or in labour as France may be induced to accept, the net result will be a smaller immediate yield than would have been obtained, if the large deferred portion of the indemnity had been omitted from the account.

While the fixation of the total obligation corrects the deep inherent vice of the provision under Annex II of the Treaty, in which three Bond Issues amounting to £5,000,000,000 are treated as " a first instalment " of an unnamed illimitable total, it does not go far towards meeting the radical objection to any assessment which exceeds the reasonable capacity to pay. The smaller limited impossibility of the present aggregate sum is as disabling a factor in its bearing upon the provision for immediate restoration as the larger unlimited impossibility of Annex II under the Treaty. For it does not matter how much greater one burden is than another, if you cannot in any event bear either of the two.

And this is the actual situation of Germany under reparation proposals based on damages and not upon capacity.

If the demands had been confined to the two first issues, and they had been distributed over a larger period instead of being demanded within this year, it is possible that Germany might have been able to defray the expenses of their service. But while the first vice of the new demands consists in the piling on of these deferred bogus billions, the second consists in the excessive size of the immediate sums required for service of the first two issues. Although the Paris proposals, with their rapid climb to a height of some £400,000,000 per annum at the eleventh year, were more intolerable in their final incidence, the new London scheme imposes a considerably heavier load at the start. This is made manifest in the addition of a 26 per cent. export duty, instead of a 12 per cent., as in the Paris terms, to the same fixed demand of £100,000,000 for the first two years. For since it is impossible that an export surplus of £100,000,000 should be provided from a total export value of less than £300,000,000, the additional duty on that amount would reach £78,000,000, making a total of £178,000,000 for the opening years. But the payment of this enlarged sum in export surplus (the only possible form of payment) must, raising that sum above £300,000,000, raise also the yield of the 26 per cent. duty. Thus it is evident that the Allied demand begins at a yearly sum of nearly £200,000,000.

Now, while it is generally agreed that Germany, with her Silesian and Ruhr mines intact, and restored facilities to foreign trade, could in due course of time restore her industries to such a level as, with economy of internal administration, would enable her to pay a considerable annual sum, no one could make a reasonable case for her ability to pay at the outset a sum approaching £200,000,000 out of her immediately available resources. I am at a loss to understand how the Reparation Commission, instructed by the Treaty to " consider the resources and capacity of Germany," can have advised the Allied Governments that Germany possesses an immediate power to pay these annual sums. For though the Commission " shall not be bound by any particular code or rules of law or by any particular rule of evidence or of procedure," it is to employ " trustworthy modes of computation."

As we proceed to cite the relevant facts regarding Germany's present capacity to pay, it will appear incredible that the Commission should have endeavoured to apply " trustworthy modes of computation," if it is upon this advice that the Allied Governments are acting. The whole procedure of presenting these demands in the shape of an ultimatum, without even giving the German Government that " just opportunity to be heard " which Article 234 requires, reduces to the merest mockery the language of the Treaty, with its grave announcement that the actions of the Commission are to be " guided by justice, equity and good faith."

The inability of Germany to fulfil these early undertakings forced upon their acceptance is so manifest that it is impossible to suppose the Allied statesmen to be ignorant of this inability. If so, we must conclude that some of them desire the natural and necessary effect of their conduct, viz., to prepare the way for early defaults upon the part of Germany, and to keep open this running sore in the body politic of Europe in order to pursue other ends which they prefer to a reasonable settlement on reparations.

IV

CAPACITY TO PAY

THE brunt of my criticism of the Allied policy on reparation turns upon the absence of any impartial investigation of Germany's capacity to pay. But the objection may be raised that, though the action of the Commission and of the Council is *ex parte*, their interest lies so clearly in the direction of securing the largest quantity of reparation actually attainable, that it is unreasonable to impute to them a policy which kills the goose that is to lay the golden eggs. Even a partial tribunal may judge fairly, if fairness is essential to the attainment of its selfish end. This may be the plea of those who hold that Germany can pay, that she is shamming poor, and that the uncompromising action of the Supreme Council is necessary to " call her bluff."

But while it may be conceded that capacity to pay is not for any nation a closely calculable sum, but one possessing a considerable elasticity, there exists a body of relevant facts and figures enabling us to reach a reasonably just estimate.

Theoretically, the capacity to pay possessed in a given year by the income of a nation consists in and is measured by the excess of that income over and above the costs of maintaining the capital and labour engaged in necessary industries and commerce, and of maintaining the necessary expenses of government. If a larger period than a single year be taken, the maximum capacity will, however, require an allowance for some saving and enlargement of capital to be made in addition to bare costs of maintenance, so that the enhanced productivity of a progressive industry may fructify in increased surplus, available for future reparation. Put otherwise, the theoretic maximum payment consists of the economic rent, surplus profits, excessive interest and salaries, the payment of which to their German recipients is not necessary in order to evoke and maintain any productive service on their part. Labour must be maintained at a level of working efficiency, capital must not be let down or discouraged from coming into being : but all income beyond these necessary payments, the surplus income of the rich and middling classes, can be taken by taxation, and, after deduction has been made for necessary costs of government, the rest can be converted into export goods for payment of reparation.

Such is the economic theory. It requires, however, several important qualifications from the practical side. No process of taxation, however searching, honest, and efficiently conducted, can secure the whole, or nearly the whole, of the theoretically attainable surplus. Every art of concealment will be employed by owners. Much of the unearned income is so closely associated with earned and necessary income as to be incapable of measurement and separation. Where properties bearing unearned or excessive incomes have been free subjects of recent transfer, at prices which discount this excess, any attack upon the present incomes they yield will arouse a passionate resentment against confiscation. In general, it is politically impracticable to effect a sudden increase of taxation beyond a certain rate, especially for such an unpopular purpose as reparation. In these and other ways the taxing power, even of the strongest and most respected State, is restricted. In the case of Germany, subjected so recently to great constitutional upheavals, it is unreasonable to expect that any Government, whether acting on its own free initiative, or still less when submitting to detailed dictation of foreign Powers, can approach the maximum surplus income through any process of taxation. The common motive, sedulously sown by the baser of the Allied statesmen, that Germany was not taxing her people as highly as some Allied countries, ought to have received its *coup de grâce* from the Report of our Commercial Secretaries at Berlin and Cologne to our Government last January, in which the estimate was given that the Reich and the State taxation for the current year would amount to 43 per cent. of the national income. Nor is there any ground for the reckless assertion that the high taxes are not collected. In addition to the burden of their regular taxation a capital levy has been imposed, and some further indirect taxation has been announced.

Out of this higher taxation, how much can be diverted into reparation remains uncertain. Against a large reduction in military and naval expenditure must be set an enormous war-pension item, which cannot, like the internal war-debt, admit either of repudiation or postponement. Moreover, though there is no public external debt to be defrayed, the aggregate indebtedness of German nationals to foreigners, the accumulation of war-advances, is very large, estimated by German officials[1] at 50 billion marks. There may be grounds for holding that Germany has abstained from reductions in some departments of her public expenditure in order to support her plea of inability to pay. But it is evident that a large proportion of her taxable capacity must be allocated to her own needs of government.

But whatever proportion of the surplus income (rents of junker landlords, town rents, high profits of cartaels and other lucrative businesses, etc.) is obtainable by taxation, must suffer a very large deduction when it is translated into the export goods by which alone reparation can be paid. For the process I here describe is one that changes the luxurious goods and services, upon which the rich classes in Germany expended most of their " unearned " incomes, together with the unnecessary comforts of the fairly prosperous middle classes and the cheaper enjoyments of the working classes, into the sort of goods which can get marketed in foreign countries. Reflection will show that the transference can only be compassed at the cost of an enormous shrinkage in values. Concretely stated, the capital, ability, and labour, which formerly went to produce goods and services of very various sorts accommodated to the luxurious or other personal requirements of different classes of the German people in their several localities, must be transferred into a comparatively restricted number of trades working for the foreign markets. Such transfer is manifestly an expensive process in itself, and can yield at first no appreciable gains, though in the process of years these export trades, fed with new supplies of labour and capital, would produce greatly enhanced quantities of those chemicals, and other scientific products, standardized metal and textile wares, ships, engines, toys and other cheap luxuries, which every Allied nation is struggling to exclude by setting up protective tariffs and other obstacles to German competition.

[1] Memorandum on Germany's solvency for the purpose of reparation, p. 13.

V

ALLIED OBSTACLES TO REPARATIONS

ENORMOUS powers are assigned to the Reparation Commission
to determine not merely how much Germany shall pay, but in what
forms payment shall be made, to decide how much foods and
materials are necessary to her in the years of reconstruction, and
to supervise and regulate both her taxing system and her internal
public expenditure, with a view to securing that, after certain
primary internal needs are satisfied, reparation shall have a first
claim on the resources of the nation. These amount in effect to
a right of arbitrary supervision over the entire economic system,
public and private, of Germany. This power of economic supervision is confirmed by a similarly compulsory power over legislation,
conveyed in Article 241 in the peremptory form that " Germany
undertakes to pass, issue, and maintain in force any legislation,
orders, and decrees, that may be necessary to give complete effect
to those provisions," the " necessity " to be determined by the
Reparation Commission.

It may, of course, be argued that no detriment is likely to
occur to the economy of Germany by the exercise of any such
powers of interference, however wide, because it is obviously to
the interest of the Allies, as recipients of reparation, so to exercise
these powers as to enable Germany to attain such industrial,
commercial, and financial efficiency as would facilitate such
payment.

There are, however, two faults in such an argument. The
first is a fault of ignorance and incompetency. Outside interference
with the delicate mechanism of national industry and public finance
is certain to be injurious, however well-intentioned it might be.
The second is the danger that the supposed interest, true or false,
of one or other the Allied States, or their nationals, would
continually deflect the control of the Commission from its primary
and avowed purpose, that of getting reparation. This injurious
tendency is admittedly responsible for many of the Treaty provisions
which cripple Germany's industrial and commercial recovery. A
report from the Port, Waterways and Railways Commission to
the Supreme Council on June 9, 1918, in reply to the German
claim for immediate reciprocity, cites two reasons for refusal.
The first is that non-reciprocity for a limited period is desirable

in order to prevent Germany from profiting from the devastation and ruin for which she was responsible. The second, closely related to the first, is the need to provide against the danger lest the land-locked states which had gained their economic independence should fall once again under the economic tutelage of Germany.[1]

Other motives are assigned by the Powers for their political and economic policy in the Saar, and for non-reciprocal conditions in the matter of commercial exchanges. The Saar policy is defended not merely as " a security for Reparation," but as " a definite and exemplary retribution " (i.e. for the destruction of French mines), while commercial non-reciprocity is " a measure of reparation " due to " a consideration of justice." [2] Such " punishment," it is urged, is " a conception which is essential to any just settlement."

The fullest avowal of this policy is contained in the Reply of the Allied and Assembled Powers, June 16, 1918,[3] directed to answer the German plea for the fulfilment of President Wilson's third " Point," viz., " The removal, so far as possible, of all economic barriers and the establishment of an equality of trade conditions among all the nations consenting to the peace and associating themselves for its maintenance." This Reply contends, first, that non-reciprocity and inequality for " a transitory period " does not really violate this point, inasmuch as the war has left certain nations in a temporary state of feebleness. Equality requires a recognition of the existing differences of economic strength and industrial integrity of the peoples of Europe. Wilson's requirement must, therefore, involve that Germany shall temporarily be deprived of the right she claims to be treated on a basis of complete equality with other nations. " The illegal acts of the enemy have placed many of the Allied States in a position of economic inferiority to Germany." " For such countries a certain freedom of action during the period of transition is vitally necessary. It is therefore a consideration for justice which has led the . . . Powers to impose on Germany, for a minimum period of four years, non-reciprocal conditions in the matter of commercial exchanges." [4] In a word, " it is only justice that restitution should be made, and that these wronged peoples should be safeguarded for a time from the competition of a nation whose industries are intact." [5]

The economic clauses of the Treaty are permeated with these

---

[1] *History of the Peace Conference*, vol. ii, p. 99.
[2] Ibid., vol. ii, p. 400, also pp. 279–389.
[3] Ibid., p. 320.
[4] Ibid., vol. ii, p. 322.
[5] Ibid., p. 376.

motives of punitive justice and provisions against the too rapid recovery of Germany's industry and commerce.

The full bearing of this upon the economic policy of reparation is, however, best understood when it is related to the commercial and fiscal conduct of the several Allied Nations after the armistice and the peace. That conduct, in accordance with the resolutions adopted by the Economic Conference at Paris in 1916, is applied, partly by legislation, partly by administrative discretion, to a policy gravely detrimental to the economic recovery of Germany, and particularly to her capacity for reparation. It is in general a graded policy of exclusion, by which each nation (1) protects its home industries against foreign competition from any source, while, by its colonial administration, it monopolizes the trade and raw materials of the empire; (2) by particular agreements with certain Allies, gives more favourable terms to the imports of their goods and a participation in the probable development of oil and other natural resources in mandatory or other subject territories; (3) imposes a protective tariff upon a higher level against imports from minor allies and neutrals; (4) directs special measures of discrimination or exclusion against important classes of German imports, accompanied by numerous disabilities or prohibitions upon their traders and settlers, and their business undertakings in allied countries and their possessions, protectorates, or mandatory areas.

The different Allies have taken different measures for developing this policy, but with the same general purpose and the same result, that of placing strong barriers against the resumption of profitable trade by Germany. The fact that linked with this purpose is the wider one of conserving, each its own national resources and markets for its own nationals, only serves to emphasize the destructive nature of the whole trade policy.

The truth is that the problem of Reparation has focused more powerfully than ever before the antagonism between the two conceptions of international trade, that which regards it as the widest form of that co-operation by division and specialization of labour which affords the greatest yield of wealth to the entire community and its particular members, and that which sees in it a conflict of activities and interests by which the members of one nation may, through governmental action, benefit themselves at the cost of the members of another nation.

All the reasoning adduced to support the various provisions for reparation in kind, non-reciprocity, forcible intervention in the economic administration of Germany, restrictions on her import and export trade, uprooting her foreign settlements and confiscation of her foreign resources, is subject to this common reprobation, that it assumes a fundamentally false conception of the nature of international economic relations.

It is, of course, true that some of the motives adduced for certain of these hostile measures are avowedly non-commercial, being punitive, compensatory, or merely precautionary. But in these cases it is never realized that the indulgence of each of these motives must be paid for in terms of reduced productivity of Germany, and therefore in reduced capacity for reparation. It is not realized that each blow struck at the enemy through these acts of peace recoils upon the striker.

All these provisions are recognized by economists in every country to be commercially unsound in their bearing upon Germany's capacity to pay and upon Europe's general capacity for economic recovery. One aspect of the complicated folly is, indeed, drilling its way into the intelligence of many members of the Allied peoples, viz., the flat contradiction between the policy of demanding a huge unnamed indemnity and the policy of keeping out the German goods, by which alone the payment of any indemnity is possible. When this education has gone further, it will expose the similar folly of all the other vexatious interferences with the revival of German industry and commerce.

If the Allies had from the first been animated by the clear dominant purpose of setting the German people to work at once under conditions enabling them to make the largest and the earliest reparation for the injuries they had inflicted, the economic policy they would have adopted would have been as follows. Recognizing that, from 1916 onward, the working population of the country had been underfed, that all industries dependent on outside raw materials had been starved, that its transport had been grievously impaired, that its credit for external purchases was wellnigh depleted, they would have striven in every way to restore the fabric of its industry and the transport system, to repair its damaged agriculture, to build up by large food supplies the economic efficiency of the population, and to furnish such additional credit as was required to make the necessary external purchases until the normal machinery of exchange was restored. Having in view these essentials of recovery, they would have been careful to secure (1) that the political and territorial changes which they made should be accompanied by as little disturbance as possible of former economic relations between the severed parts, and that, in particular, political severance should entail no fiscal or transport barriers ; (2) that, having regard to the fact that every European nation was more or less suffering from a shortage of food, fuel, raw materials, machinery, and manufactured goods, the provisions of the Treaties and the post-war policy should be directed to secure for all nations the utmost freedom of importation and exportation consistent with sumptuary regulations.

The intrusion of motives hostile to this sound economy, whether protectionist, fiscal, imperialist, punitive, or predatory, has made the collective and social policy of the Allies one of economic strangulation. Instead of co-operating in an effective international arrangement for the restoration of Europe, by apportioning short supplies of essentials to accord with national needs, each nation has set about conserving its supplies for its exclusive use, and erecting new barriers of commerce, primarily intended to weaken and retard the recovery of their ex-enemies, but also animated by a fresh impulse of national self-sufficiency, the economic backstroke of the fears, hates, suspicions, jealousies and greeds, which the war had fostered.

These economic faults and follies have contributed to cripple the recovery of the ex-enemy countries, to impair their powers of reparation, and by a necessary implication to hamper the industry, commerce, and finance of the Allies, other European countries, and the entire world.

VI

THE EXPORT SURPLUS

HAVING regard to the loss of territory and of internal and external resources to which she has been subjected, and to the various other restrictions, prohibitions, and disabilities contained in the Peace Treaties and the post-war policy, what is the reasonable amount of reparation Germany should be asked to pay, and how should it be distributed in time ? Or, alternatively, given such revision of the Treaty and of the Allied policy as will, so far as possible, remove these obstacles and disabilities, what amount of reparation might be got under these improved conditions ?

Starting from the two admitted premises that, before any capacity for reparation exists, the necessary livelihood of the German population must be assured, and that it is undesirable to extend the period during which reparation is paid beyond thirty years, we soon reach the governing condition of our inquiry, viz., the admission that the reparation must be paid in terms of the surplus of export over import trade, an annual payment. The acknowledgment of this time-limit carries this important implication. It rules out the acquisition by foreigners of any large ownership of property in Germany as a mode of reparation. For such ownership, were it not cancelled before a generation had elapsed, would involve what would amount to a continuation of the payment of reparation beyond that period. Therefore, however desirable it may be that Germany's early capacity to pay should be facilitated and increased by the temporary mortgage of her capital resources to foreigners, such advances should not form a permanent burden upon the German population. This serves to enforce the central thesis that the amount of German reparation must be presented in terms of annual export surpluses.

Now Germany's foreign trade, on an average of the five years ending 1913, showed an excess of imports over visible exports to the extent of £74,000,000. This import surplus was balanced by means of interest upon existing foreign securities, profits of shipping, foreign banking, trading, etc., the sum of which exceeded this balance, allowing a considerable sum for further foreign investments. The whole of these " invisible exports " having, however, been destroyed by the terms of the peace and the post-war Allied policy, Germany's pre-war foreign commerce, were it otherwise completely resumable, could furnish no surplus whatever for reparation. On the contrary, so far from having an export surplus she would have a deficit, unable to pay for what she sought to buy. This deficit would be enhanced by the fact that the war has converted Germany from being a creditor nation, having annual interest to receive from foreigners, into a debtor nation having annual interest to pay. From the beginning of the war to February 1920 it has been estimated [1] that the balance of imports over exports amounts to about 60 billions marks, and that after allowing for the payment of 4½ billions by export of gold, and 5·6 billions by sale of securities, a total foreign debt of some 50 billions remains to be financed out of the annual income of the country. Whatever allowance be made for exaggeration in this German estimate, it remains true that in order to make any payment to the Allies she must either greatly increase her exports or reduce her imports, or do both.

Now how far do the new economic conditions enable her to perform successfully either of these processes ?

An analysis of Germany's import trade for 1913 [2] shows that

[1] Memorandum on Germany's solvency for the purpose of reparation, p. 12.
[2] Cf. Keynes' *Economic Consequences of the Peace*, pp. 190-2.

it consisted to the extent of 35·3 per cent. of raw materials for manufacture of articles for domestic use or for export, 28·3 per cent. of foodstuffs, for the most part cereals, oils, cattle, and other necessary foods, while 3·9 per cent. consisted of semi-manufactured textiles and machinery. Of the remaining 32·5 per cent. the great bulk consisted either of articles of consumption, contributing to the subsistence and working efficiency of the German people, or of capital goods serviceable for the production of such necessaries or of export goods. In other words, no large percentage of imports consisted of luxuries or other non-productive consumption, the only part of import trade that could be dispensed with advantageously. Assume that 10 per cent. of the 1913 imports could be thus ranked as " unproductive," the reduction would amount in pre-war values to some £53,000,000, or in post-war gold values to some £90,000,000.

Now turn to the export side in order to consider how exports can be increased. In 1913 not less than 27·7 per cent. of the export consisted of iron goods, machinery, and coal. The loss of territory supplying three-quarters of her iron ore, 38 per cent. of her blast-furnaces, 9 per cent. of her foundries, 9 per cent. of her coal-mines, and the coal payments under the Spa Agreement (or 32 per cent. if Upper Silesia goes to Poland), must greatly diminish her capacity for exporting this class of goods, as well as others in which coal and iron enter largely as costs of production. If, as is contended sometimes, Germans will be able to buy coal and iron from other countries to make up these losses, the necessity of paying for such external supplies in more export goods only transfers, and does not lighten, the difficulty. Next in importance to iron and coal come cotton and woollen goods, comprising 11·5 per cent. in 1913, leather, sugar, paper, furs, electrical goods, dyes, copper goods, toys, rubber and rubber goods, books, maps and music, potash, glass, potassium-chloride, pianos, organs and parts, raw zinc, porcelain. These compose in all two-thirds of the export values. They fall in the main into three classes : (1) essential goods, based upon superior scientific processes ; (2) cheap standardized metal and textile goods ; (3) luxury and artistic goods. What are the prospects of a greatly increased export trade in any of these classes, under such conditions as to earn a large gold income ? Will the Allied countries, who took so large a share of these exports before the war, increase their purchase ? Apart from the general reluctance of their populations to buy any goods from Germany, the fiscal policies of most of the Allies are directed against the admission into their markets of each of those three classes. Britain, for example, has passed legislation designed to keep out most important items of Class I as "key industries" and large sections of Class II as "dumped goods," while both her general protective and her sumptuary policy must tend to cut down Class III to the narrowest dimensions. A small proportion of Germany's pre-war export trade consisted of articles made exclusively from German materials (therefore involving no increased import trade), and not exposed to the objections cited above.[1]

The entire medley of the Allied post-war policy, peace terms, tariffs, embargoes and prohibitions, unnamed reparation, has, in a word, contributed to reduce the export power of Germany, thus disabling her for reparation. For, quite apart from the obstacles thus placed in the way of production, transport and marketing of export goods, the low, fluctuating and unpredictable exchange, which these conditions have helped to bring about, has a constricting influence on her export trade. The fatuity of the Allied attitude towards reparation reaches its zenith in the tariff regulations taken by their respective Governments to correct the effect of the bad exchange of Germany in enabling her exporters to pour cheap-priced goods into their markets. For, first, in default of the free export of gold (now out of the question), such flows of goods are the only possible way in which a bad exchange can be corrected. Secondly, they are the only way in which reparation can be provided. Reparation in terms of German labour was refused by France after elaborate provisions had actually been drafted for its provision in the Versailles Treaty, and though the new London scheme reverts to the idea, it is tolerably certain that French labour will be strong enough to stop any large contribution from this source. Germany's other proposal in 1919 to give payment in the shape of investments in German industrial enterprises was also refused by the Allies, "because," according to Mr. Dulles, "it was regarded as a device to ensure the Allied peoples becoming so bound up in the internal affairs of Germany and so sympathetic towards the prompt economic revival and prosperity of Germany, that the Allied Governments would be embarrassed in their political relations with Germany."[2] But in any case, as I have pointed out, the real reparation thus furnished must take shape in the German exports representing interest on their investments.

Since the German reparation is made in gold marks, it might have been supposed that the lower the prices at which, owing to

[1] Cf. *History*, vol. ii, p. 50, for a computation of the pre-war surplus of exports.
[2] Address in New York, March 12, 1921.

the bad exchange, German goods could pour into Allied markets, the greater the quantity of real reparation. The chief aim and result, therefore, of the duty in our recent Tariff Act upon goods entering our markets from countries of low exchange, is by raising the price and reducing the quantity of German goods imported into our country, to diminish the real reparation as much as possible. By pursuing this policy far enough, and by co-operation with our Allies, we should enable Germany to pay the total reparation in the smallest quantity of real wealth, though necessarily spread over the longest period of years.

This, indeed, may be described as " the logic " of the Allied policy on reparations, the resultant of the two sets of forces, one making for the largest and most impossible demands for payment in gold marks, the other for the most strenuous refusal to receive the only sorts of goods by which these gold marks can be earned.

To this *impasse*, however, there is a further contribution from the same source. The refusal to enable Germany to correct the bad exchange by her large export trades continues to disable her from buying ahead the raw materials which she must require in increasing quantities for the performance of her reparation task in the only way it can be performed. Any impartial observer of the situation would undoubtedly conclude from the accumulation of obstacles set in the only path of reparation that the Allied Governments wished to receive from Germany the least possible amount of reparation.

Any close consideration of the specific reactions of the Allied post-war policy upon German productivity in general strengthens this analysis of her export disabilities. The effective supplies of labour, capital, business ability, science and intellectual equipment, all vital elements in productivity, have all sustained heavy damages through the war, the blockade, the peace terms, and the post-war economic policy of the Allies. A people, reduced in number by some nine millions through loss of territory, the remainder reduced in number by the loss of some two millions slain and another million permanently disabled, the entire working population damaged in vitality and working efficiency by privations which will sap the productivity of the rising generation—such are the heavy losses of the productive power of labour. Even graver are the damages inflicted on the brain-workers, upon whose efficiency the burden of industrial progress chiefly rests. Not merely have the professional, artistic, and intellectual classes sustained, as individuals, economic damages to their standard of living that have impaired their productive powers, but the public insolvency threatens to destroy the collective foundations of education and of culture. Business enterprise and initiative are deprived of their necessary stimuli : personal economy, thrift, saving for the maintenance and improvement of the capital structure of industry are all alike inhibited by a sense of insecurity about the future and the fear lest successful industry may merely serve to swell the volume of indemnity.

This combination of concrete obstacles with psychological deterrents, all operating through degraded currency to paralyse effective recovery and progress of German industry and commerce, renders it impossible that the total yield of German real income should be such as to furnish the requisite surplus of exports to pay a large gold mark reparation, after the prior charges for the necessary provision for the maintenance of the German population, the upkeep of its Government, and the cost of the armies of occupation, have been taken into account.

In concluding this analysis of the problem of reparation, specific reference must be made to what may be called " the state of mind " of Germany in its distinctively economic bearing. The frequently expressed judgment of Allied spokesmen that the German people ought to recognize their sole responsibility for the war and to feel a keen sense of penitence, coupled with a desire to make a reparation on the score of justice, need not here be discussed in relation to its objective truth. It must suffice to say that there is not the least likelihood of the German people accepting as effective incentives towards reparation any such judgment. On the contrary, it is natural that, as the Allies dwell upon the guilt and cruelty of Germany in the causation and conduct of the war, Germans should see in that war a policy of their enemies carried into consummation in the guilt and cruelty of the peace. These sentiments, whether justified or not, must exercise a depressing influence upon the processes of economic recuperation, inducing in the more sensitive sections of the population a feeling either of futile irritability or sheer torpor, and in either case a lowering of moral energy exceedingly injurious to productive effort.

.   .   .   .   .   .

The aggregate effect of these considerations upon the solution of the problem of reparation cannot be expressed in any quantitative terms. But it is indisputably true that the net effect of these injurious influences upon current German productivity and foreign commerce, if maintained, is such that no substantial reparation can be made, except by methods (e.g. the forcible removal of coal, gold, etc.) which, in order to effect some small immediate payment, let down injuriously the subsistence of the population and impair the recovery and progress of the economic system of the country.

The only way in which any substantial reparation can be got is by adopting a policy expressly directed to restore Germany as soon and as completely as possible to the highest pitch of productivity and the fullest liberty of foreign trade to which her injured and diminished natural and human resources are capable of attaining. If some of the disabling mischief cannot be undone, every effort should be made to repair the disabilities.

This sound policy of reparation would involve :—

1. Cancelment of all the injurious clauses in the economic and financial sections of the Treaty, as well as in those provisions of the Reparation Section, to which we have referred.

2. A removal of all prohibitions, discriminations, and other restrictions upon the transport and foreign trade between Germany and other countries imposed by the post-war policy of the several Allies.

3. The provision of such positive assistance in the shape of transport, coal, and credit, as would enable the German people to restore their damaged industry and set their internal and external finances upon such a footing as would conduce to the highest productivity and the largest export trade with the greatest celerity.

4. The removal of the entire issue from the *ex-parte* judgment of the Supreme Council and the Commission to an impartial Commission of Neutrals with a view to the fixation as soon as possible, of such a sum of reparation as under these improved circumstances it is reasonably estimated Germany can afford to pay within a generation, without letting down the population and the future productivity, and such as the Allies can afford to receive without injurious reaction upon their economic system.

Milton Keynes UK
Ingram Content Group UK Ltd.
UKHW040638310823
427678UK00018B/309

9 781528 715010